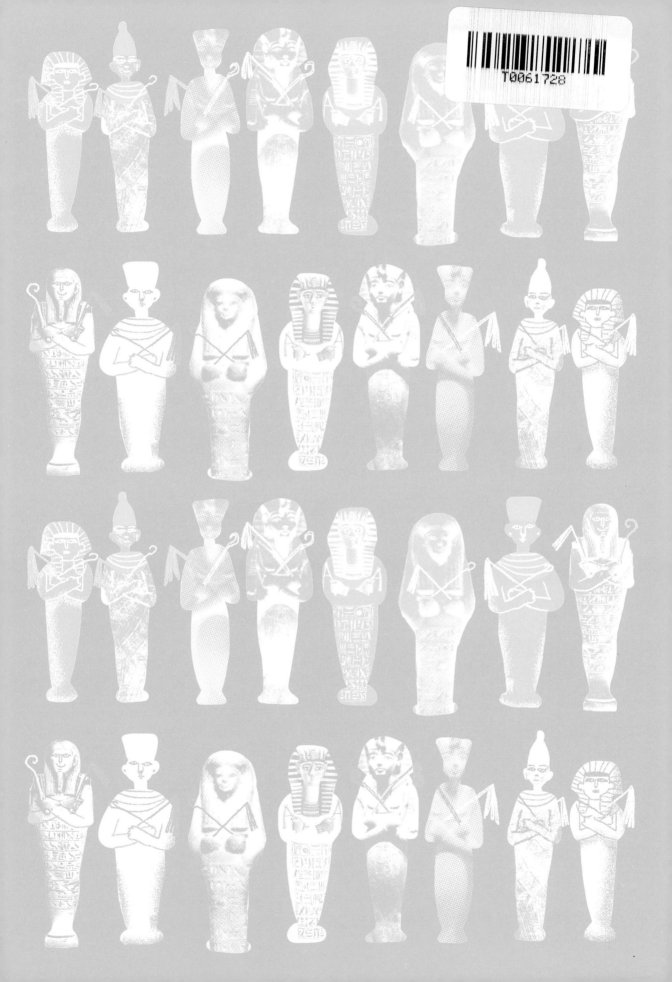

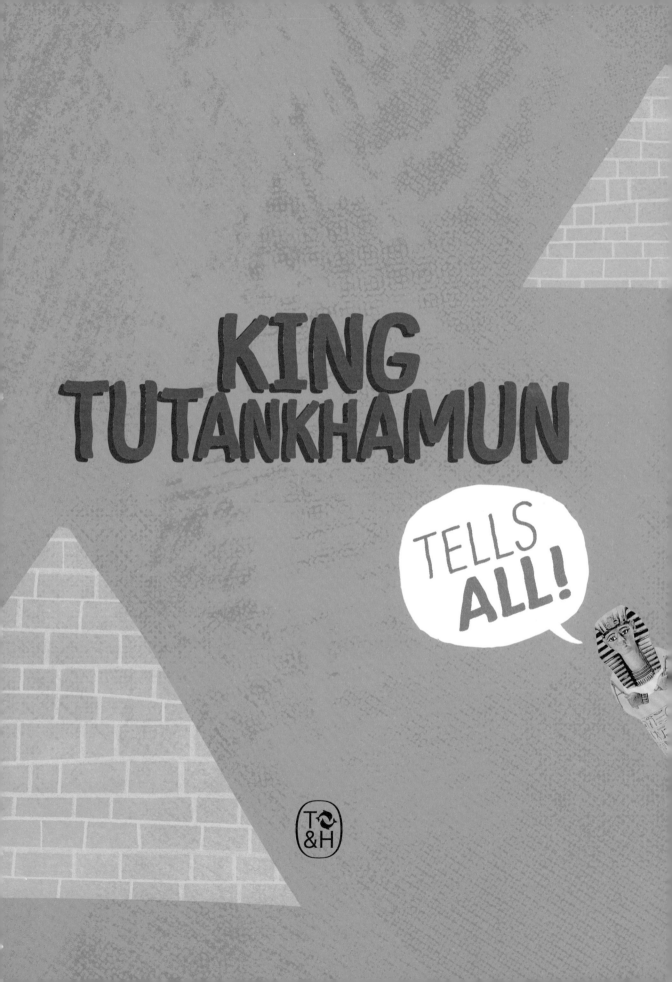

KING TUTANKHAMUN

TELLS ALL!

T&H

For Ciarán – C.N.

To my boys Lucca and Vicente,
you are my real treasure! – G.K.

KING TUTANKHAMUN

TELLS ALL!

Chris Naunton

Illustrated by
Guilherme Karsten

CONTENTS

THE TOMB OF
KING TUTANKHAMUN
1323 BCE

This spectacular coffin dates back to the 18th Dynasty in ancient Egypt. It contains the mummified remains of the boy king, Tutankhamun, who died at the young age of 18. He is seen here surrounded by shabtis. "Shabti" means "answerer."

These shabtis are figurines of the king and were believed to do his work for him in the afterlife. The Book of the Dead mentions the formula you need to use to get them working: "Oh shabti, if I have to do any work in the afterlife, you will do it for me. You'll say, 'Here I am!'"

Epic! Imagine having little minions like these to do your work for you. Hey, shabti—HERE I AM! I have some chores for you to help me with and a little sister who needs babysitting.

Excuse me! Those are MY shabtis, and they are plenty busy keeping little so-and-sos like you from disturbing me in my afterlife.

AAARGHHH! He's ALIVE!!!

HELLO, I'M KING TUTANKHAMUN

Dear Readers,

You may know me from such epic tales as Howard Carter's digging up of the Valley of the Kings, Tomb Raiders, and other exciting adventures. Welcome to my afterlife.

Since my early death in 1323 BCE, I have had a constant flow of visitors: tourists taking selfies; Egyptologists prodding me; and young children with too many questions, interrupting what is supposed to be my quiet time, meditating on how I'm going to be reborn. Hardly fit for a king is it?

In the pages that follow I will relay the incredible, unbelievable and remarkable details of my life in ancient Egypt—in my own words. You'll laugh, you'll cry, you'll bow down and worship me. Because I am none other than the pharaoh, Tutankhamun.

Yours,
Tut xx

ONCE UPON A TIME IN...
ANCIENT EGYPT

Even though I'm only a teenager, the people of Egypt *fear me*. I am the king of all kings and rule the **richest** kingdom on Earth. This is how we roll...

SUMMER ALL YEAR ROUND

My family has lived in and around the Sahara desert for centuries. It's summer 24/7. Our palaces and temples are designed to be super chill and all our air conditioning comes from renewable sources (by which I mean servants).

RIVERSIDE LIVING

Besides the lovely view, living next to the Nile River has many benefits. When the river floods, it waters the farmers' fields for free, making food crops easy to grow.

CONSTRUCTION WORKERS ON TAP

Every year the Nile floods and fertilizes the earth. To keep farmers busy while their fields were flooded, my ancestors got them to drag 2 million blocks of stone into the middle of the desert. See that pyramid? It took 50,000 people 20 years to build. No sweat!

RICHER THAN BILL GATES

We may not have money in ancient Egypt, but that doesn't mean we aren't extremely flush. I am so rich, I never have to wear the same pair of shoes twice. Elon Musk and Jeff Bezos, eat my dust.

HOW I BECOME THE BOY KING

My family is **bonkers**. We have ruled Egypt for **centuries**, which is stressful enough. The events that lead to me being crowned king at the **age of 9** are by no means ordinary...

① GRANDPA DIES

Pharaoh Amenhotep III, my grandpa, dies before I am even born (he built some incredible stuff—have you been to Luxor Temple in Thebes?) Pharoah Akhenaten takes over. I'm not sure if Akhenaten was actually my father, but I like to call him "Dad" anyway.

② WE ALL MOVE

So far so good...until Dad decides to build a completely new city called Akhetaten (which you now call "Amarna"). He relocates our family and the entire population of Thebes there—Grandma Tiye included.

③ GRANDMA GETS SICK

My Grandma Tiye is amazing, if a bit fierce. A lot of people don't like her, but she is my favorite family member (I still have some of her hair in a box). So when Grandma falls ill, it comes as a shock.

④ NO ROOM IN THE TOMB

When Grandma dies, Dad is like, "Well, I want her to be buried in my tomb, here in Amarna." His builder, Hatiay, is like, "Hate to break it to you, but we haven't built a space for her." And Dad is like, "Well, she's my mom and I'm the king so you're going to have to figure this out."

⑤ GRANDMA IS ACTUALLY DEAD

So, they make a space in the Royal Tomb for Grandma Tiye right next to where Dad is going to lie. They decorate it with carvings of people weeping and Grandma is nested into multiple shrines, like a Russian doll. And that's when it hits me—Grandma is actually dead.

6 DAD JOINS A CULT

Did I mention that Dad decided to change our religion too? Before he moved our entire population to a brand-new city, he invented a new cult and got everyone to worship Aten, the sun disc. Everyone's favorite gods, Amun and Mut, felt a bit neglected. So when Dad dies, everyone lets out a sigh of relief. After all, the gods are far more powerful than any king, even me!

HELLO
my name is
~~NEFERTITI~~

NEFERNEFERUATEN

7 MOM HAS A MID-LIFE CRISIS

After Dad dies, my stepmom Neferneferuaten-Nefertiti takes over and has a crisis of confidence. She shortens her name to "Neferneferuaten," which includes the name of "Aten." She wants everyone to know that our god wants her to be queen—it isn't just because everyone else went and died.

8 WE ALL MOVE BACK TO THEBES

People start telling Neferneferuaten she should put everything back to how it was. So she starts packing and moves us back to Thebes. But somehow Dad and Grandma's mummies get left behind... (I think it just slipped her mind).

THEBES

after life REMOVAL

⑨ I BECOME KING, AGE 9

Then Neferneferuaten dies and I become king. I AM ONLY NINE! I can't stop thinking about Dad and Grandma being left behind, so I decide to go and get them.

⑩ WE BECOME LESS POPULAR

By the time I'm king, Dad has become really unpopular. All the priests who had been saying "Yes sir, no sir" when he was alive start saying that they never liked his new ways! When I relocate the tombs of Dad and Grandma to Thebes, I have to be careful. I mark everything with my royal seal to make sure no one touches anything.

⑪ SOMEONE STEALS GRANDMA

Dad and Grandma are now in a little tomb in the Valley of the Kings, with as many of their belongings as I can fit in. But can you believe it: someone sneaks in, steals everything valuable, unwraps Grandma and puts her in another tomb! She is not impressed.

HOW DARE THEY!

15

I RULE

In case you haven't yet grasped, I am the ruler of the whole wide world. Well, the world as I know it. My advice? Let your ancestors and enemies do the work for you.

LET YOUR GRANDPA DO THE CONQUERING

My ancestors did a lot of conquering—especially my great, great, great-grandpa Thutmose III. He started by conquering a kingdom to the east of Egypt called Naharin and just kept going. By the time he'd finished, he'd conquered 350 cities in parts of modern-day Palestine, Israel, Jordan, Lebanon, Syria, Iraq and Turkey, as well as Sudan to the south of Egypt. Our empire is enormous!

STEAL FROM YOUR ENEMIES

Enemies aren't all bad, especially if you can turn them into dust and steal all their best ideas. Egypt's enemies, the Hyksos, gave us horses, chariots, slings, throwsticks and boomerangs. And the Nubians have taught us how to fight with a new kind of bow and arrow. They've helped us take over the world without even meaning to. Thanks, guys!

HEY, THAT BOW IS MINE!

DON'T FIGHT IF YOU DON'T HAVE TO

I am trained to fight, but I very rarely do. Ever since I became pharaoh, my main concern has been to restore order after the ruckus Dad caused. There are enemies to face in the afterlife too, so I figure I may as well use my time on Earth to get good without getting hurt. Besides, with violent new metal weapons like daggers now available, who wants to fight if they don't have to?!

17

MY VERY EARLY DEATH

Despite how rich and powerful I am, I'm still only human. And in my case, that means dying an early death. How do I die? Wouldn't you like to know?!

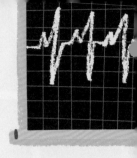

THEORY 1: **MURDER**

One anatomist thinks I am hit over the head by one of my enemies. As if I'd let my enemies get that close to me! Are you sure the hole in my skull isn't thanks to a clumsy archaeologist???

THEORY 2: **CHARIOT ACCIDENT**

A very popular theory is that I die in a chariot-riding accident, which I reject. I am a very good driver, thank you very much!

THEORY 3: CLUB FOOT

Some medical experts using genetic studies think that my death is related to having a club foot. I admit, ancient Egyptian medicine wasn't as advanced as it is today. But being born with a club foot wasn't enough to kill me...

THEORY 4: A BROKEN KNEE

Archaeologists notice that I have hurt my knee and decide that's what killed me. Have you ever hurt your knee? And did you die from it? Didn't think so!

THE ANSWER?

Mind your own business! You can keep trying to find out, but I'm not telling! We Egyptians are FAR more interested in our life on Earth and our eternal afterlife than how we die. The moment we make the change from one life to the next just isn't a big deal. Get over it!

MY BUNGLED BURIAL

Getting buried involves being wrapped up in lots of layers, like a big present. But because I die suddenly, it doesn't quite go according to plan...

1 **FIND A TOMB, QUICK!**

I had been planning a tomb much bigger than the one I'm now in. But I die before it's finished and have to be buried in someone else's. It's tiny by my standards, with only four rooms!

2

BUILD MULTIPLE COFFINS

My coffin is actually three coffins that fit neatly inside one another. First, my body is placed inside a coffin of SOLID GOLD. That is then sealed inside another wooden coffin covered with gold, which is nested inside a third coffin, also covered with gold.

❸ RECYCLE A SARCOPHAGUS

Because of my untimely death, the priests and officials in charge of my burial have chosen to use someone else's sarcophagus, or stone box. When they lower my coffin into it, they realize it's too short—my feet are poking out! What do they do? SAW OFF the end of my coffin!! I have the wood chips in the bottom of my sarcophagus to prove it!

❹ COVER WITH SHRINES

My sarcophagus is then covered with a series of golden shrines that look like huts. There are four of them altogether, each one bigger than the last.

❺ SQUEEZE INTO BURIAL CHAMBER

I am now the size of the burial chamber itself, which makes fitting inside a bit of a squeeze... There's enough room for a really skinny person to walk sideways around the edge, but that's it.

PACKING FOR THE AFTERLIFE

The **afterlife** isn't a catnap—it's *another life!* So I'm hugely relieved when my relatives cram as much as they can into my tomb. Come and see what they've packed for me...

A CAMP BED

It's not the most comfortable, but I can take my camp bed anywhere—better than sleeping on the sand right?! It's made of organically grown rope (obvs), which has been woven by hand by pitiful servants—I mean, local artisans.

WALKING STICKS

These walking sticks are apparently for when I get older. But the worst thing has happened—all the archaeologists assume I can't walk properly. I'M 18, NOT 80!!

HIGH-TECH WEAPONS

Bows, arrows, shields, blah, blah blah—nothing special. But let me show you my daggers. This one is made of IRON—have you heard of it? It's amazing stuff—super high-tech and incredibly strong. And perfect for scaring away light-fingered grave robbers...

FAST CHARIOTS

Because I'm the pharaoh, I have enemies everywhere—even in the afterlife. So I'm glad my relatives think to bury me with a suitable getaway. My chariots are decorated with pictures of my enemies tied up in ropes—sends the right message, don't you think?

23

JOURNEY TO THE AFTERLIFE

Arriving in the afterlife doesn't just happen at the snap of a finger (or neck, for that matter). It is literally a journey. Lucky for me, the murals in my burial chamber lead the way.

1 Take a deep breath

The priest who embalms your body before burial will perform magic on your mummy so you can eat, drink and breathe after you're dead. It's your spirit who will travel to the afterlife, while your mummy stays in your tomb. Your spirit might want to come back here for a rest at some point, so don't stop breathing!

2 Go and find Osiris

The afterlife is in a place called the Duat. Find the god Osiris—he has green skin and is hard to miss. Osiris will weigh your heart on some scales and judge you. Better go prepared.

❸ Follow the sun

Luckily, the people burying me put me in my tomb the right way around, with my head pointing west. Every day the sun god Ra travels across the sky from East to West. He then goes past the horizon and travels through the night on a boat. Follow that boat!

The twelve baboons in my mural tell me it will take twelve hours to get there—as long as it takes for Ra to travel through the night.

Um, why does Ra look like a beetle?

Egyptian gods can be more than one being at the same time. I'm sure you've seen a video of a beetle rolling a ball of dung across the ground? The sun is a ball too, and it's rolled across the sky each day by a scarab beetle—the sun god Ra. Confused?!

NUT + me! (awesome day!)

Here's me with Nut, goddess of the sky—such a celeb.

❹ Stay positive

The journey is long, so it's important to set off in a positive frame of mind. Based on these pictures, I've got a good feeling about it.

OSI, ME and ME (again)

That's me hugging my buddy Osiris with…another me! Actually, the second me is my ka, or spirit. While I head off to find Osiris, my ka will live on in my tomb forever.

DRESSED TO IMPRESS

I don't know where people get this idea that mummies go wandering around in the bandages they got buried in. That's just gross! If you're about to have your past life judged, you need to dress to impress.

FAVORITE T-SHIRT

Nothing says "I rule" like this tunic. It's made of linen, so it keeps me cool when I have to get angry at my servants. And the collar and edges are designs from Syria—just another little country I've "borrowed" a few ideas and riches from. I'm very cosmopolitan like that.

SERIOUS BLING

What jewelry should I wear? I've got so much, it's hard to decide! I used to love earrings when I was younger, but they're far too childish for me now. A pectoral is much more grown-up. But which one—the falcon with its wings outstretched, or the scarab beetle?

HIDDEN UNDIES

OMG! I've just realized some of my old underwear is in the tomb. How embarrassing. As long as that archaeologist Howard Carter doesn't find it— he documents EVERYTHING.

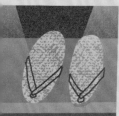

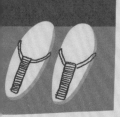

TOUGH KICKS

I LOVE shoes. I've kept every pair I've ever had since I was little. Some of them are so nice, they're barely worn. These have pictures of the enemies of Egypt under my feet— as if I'm trampling on my enemies with every step! A little rude, maybe, but it is part of my job description to conquer as many people as possible. If the shoe fits, wear it!

SPIRITUAL SECURITY

How do I stay so levelheaded even though I'm dead?
I surround myself with people I trust not to kill me—
it's possible to die twice, remember!

KEEP FAMILY CLOSE

If your family has as many enemies as mine
does, marry someone who is less likely to
stab you in your sleep, such as a sibling. I'm
married to my stepsister Akhesenamun,
who I love so much, I have her picture on
my throne. That's not so weird is it?

SEND WARNING SIGNS

All my chairs, beds and couches
are carved with lion's feet. It sends
a clear message: "Respect me or
I'll tear you apart."

BEWARE OF THE ~~DOG~~ GOD

This is my guard god, Anubis (he's
actually a wild jackal). Anubis is
in charge of mummification and
helps Osiris to judge whether you've
behaved well enough to reach the
afterlife. Eek!

"It is I who stops the sand from coming in here...
I am here to protect the dead person..."

ANCIENT BOUNCERS

You've got to love my guardian statues! They're big, they're holding maces, and they're ready to smack anyone who tries to get past them. It's just a shame they draw attention to the false wall hiding my burial chamber...

NOTHING TO SEE HERE!

How does Osiris know if I've been good?

Your heart will be weighed on a pair of scales against a feather belonging to Maat, the goddess of truth. If your heart tips the balance, it means you've been bad and you will be fed to Ammit—a monster with the hind legs of a hippo, the front legs of a leopard and the head of a crocodile.

DINING WHEN DEAD

Just because my physical stomach has been removed, it doesn't mean my ka, or spirit, won't get hungry. Who can resist a banquet like this?!

GET BURIED WITH A PRIVATE CHEF

My funerary team has done a great job of stocking up my tomb with treats, but when supplies get low, I'll simply order my shabtis to make more bread and beer from the barley and emmer grains.

EAT A HIGH-FIBER DIET

Fruits and veggies are as important in the afterlife as they are on Earth. My stash includes chickpeas, lentils and dried peas, which can be spiced up with juniper, coriander, fenugreek, sesame and cumin. For dessert? Dates, doum palm fruit, dried grapes, jujubes and almonds. Yum!

SPECIAL OF THE DAY

My funerary team labeled the forty-eight meat boxes so carefully, but somehow they got mixed up—disaster! That said, it's nice to get a surprise each time I open a new box. What will today's special be—beef, goat, duck or goose?

SWEET WINE | made by Nakhtsobek
House of Aten, Western River

POMEGRANATE WINE | made by Nakht
House of the Aten of Tajru

THE WINE LIST

Most Egyptians live on beer, but my favorite drink is more sophisticated, like me. I have more than fifty jars of wine to choose from, including some made by my personal wine maker, Kha, at the royal vineyard in Thebes.

Some idiot from England was arrogant enough to play my silver trumpet live on radio and guess what? He broke it. No wonder—it takes years to master!

Who broke the trumpet?

BACKGROUND MUSIC

Shabtis come in handy for many things. If I feel like having a lively evening in, I hand them these clappers, a sistra—like a tambourine—and trumpets, and tell them to get jiggy with it.

SPELLS FOR A HAPPY AFTERLIFE

There's a risk that some of my behavior on Earth might count against me, so I've taken the trouble to prepare some magic spells to influence the gods in my favor.

SPELLED OUT ON PAPYRUS

For some time now I've been planning a custom edition of "The Book of the Dead," written on a 20-foot-long roll of papyrus. It includes all the spells I might need to protect myself on the journey to the afterlife and to enjoy everything eternal life has to offer.

PICTURE OF PARADISE

I've selected the best scribe in the kingdom and briefed them to draw pictures of Aaru, the Field of Reeds. It's where everyone hopes to live in the afterlife, so I figure that the better my picture, the stronger my chance of securing the perfect spot in paradise.

A SPELL TO PROVE I'M PERFECT

I trust Osiris to judge me fairly, but I also want to make sure he knows how good I've been. Here's the spell I'll use when we meet:

"Hello great god! I know who you are! I've come to tell you the truth, no lying! In fact, I have never told lies, I've never made anyone else poor, I haven't done anything wrong or evil, I haven't made anyone hungry, or made anyone cry and so on and so on."

What?! No spell book?!
OMG—the priests have forgotten to bury me with my spell book! How am I going to survive the afterlife without it?!

33

MY TOMB GETS BURIED

Most people think it doesn't rain in the desert. On this occasion, the rain is heavy enough to flood the entire Valley of the Kings.

PRIME LOCATION

The Valley of the Kings is the spot in the desert where all us pharaohs are buried in one enormous royal cemetery. It's in a prime location—set away from the busy Nile River and its temples and palaces, but close to the Western Mountains, where the sun sets and Osiris lives.

BURIED AGAIN

Soon after my burial, it starts raining in the Western Mountains and floods into the valley. The door to my tomb is sealed just in time! The flood waters dump tons of stone and dust on top of the entrance to my tomb, completely burying it. Now no one knows where to find me!

CROWDING IN THE DESERT

The valley is already quite crowded, and after the flood it's even harder to tell where one tomb starts and another ends. King Sethnakht's workmen accidentally break into the tomb of King Amenmessu during the construction of a long hallway—oops! Then Ramesses VI's builders put their workers' huts right on top of my tomb, so his entrance is in the same place as my entrance.

HOWARD CARTER SHOWS UP

I've been asleep for some centuries now, enjoying my afterlife in full. So you can imagine how annoyed I am when Howard Carter digs me up in 1922.

1 THE DIGGING STARTS

In the early 1900s archaeologists start digging around the Valley of the Kings, looking for tombs. They come really close to mine but decide they've uncovered everything there is to find. Except for a British man named Howard Carter...

2 GETTING WARMER...

Mr. Carter has been coming to the valley to dig for seven years and he is specifically looking for me, which makes me nervous. First he finds some belongings of mine. Then he finds the huts on top of Ramesses VI's tomb. THEN he starts digging downward...

3 STAIRS MARK THE SPOT

On November 4, 1922, Mr. Carter and his workmen are suspiciously quiet, and I think I know why—they have found the steps leading to my tomb. They clear the rubble from the stairs and uncover the doorway.

4 DO NOT DISTURB

The doorway to my tomb is sealed. Now, most people would think that means they're not supposed to go any further—not Howard! He recognizes the signs of the royal cemetery stamped on my clay door seal and decides to open up.

5 BREAKING AND ENTERING

Howard Carter waits three weeks for his boss, Lord Carnarvon, to arrive from England before he breaks into my tomb. By this time, a crowd of Egyptian officials have gathered. They notice two things: my name is on the door in hieroglyphs, and someone has broken in before...

TOMB RAIDERS

Howard Carter wasn't the first to break into my tomb...

TOMB RAIDER 1

I had just fallen asleep when someone first broke into my tomb. They didn't stay for long—just made a bit of a noise and then left. That was before the floods hit.

TOMB RAIDER 2

My second tomb raiders took a lot of my lovely jewelry, which is easy to sell. But because they got caught, they also got punished: they had the soles of their feet beaten before being impaled on a stake—ouch!

DESIGNED TO FOOL

Tombs are designed to fool robbers. Builders create passages that go nowhere, construct rooms containing nothing, hide burial chambers like mine behind false walls and disguise entranceways with great big stones. But despite all their efforts, robbers still find a way to get in.

TOMB RAIDER 3

When Carter saw evidence of these earlier break-ins, he wasn't worried that I was missing some essential items for the afterlife. He was concerned that after years of digging, there might not be any treasure left for him. Doesn't he know how extremely rich I am?! Even after these robberies, my tomb is still loaded!

TOMB RAIDER 4

A few years after Carter finishes his work, robbers break into my tomb again and take what's left. But do you know what's worse? They damage my mummy and break my ribs! Give me a break!

6'6"
6'0"
5'6"
5'0"
4'6"
4'0"

TREASURE

I BECOME FAMOUS

Thanks to Howard Carter, I become even more famous than I was already. People from all over the world absolutely worship me!

THE NEWS TODAY

HITTING THE HEADLINES

"Remarkable Discovery in Egypt."
"New Tomb Found—Egypt's Greatest."
"Gold-Cased Mummy of Tutankhamun."
My name is splashed all over the papers.
The idea that Carter has "discovered" me
is hilarious—I knew where I was all along!

MOVIE STUD

The most popular image of me is my striking
funeral mask—and because it looks great
on camera, I become an instant movie star!
I inspire countless stories about mummies,
tomb raids and ancient Egypt.

NEXT SCREENING -THURS

THE MUMMY

TOURIST TRAP

Before Carter has even analyzed any of its contents, my tomb becomes a tourist trap, with press reporters from around the world demanding tours on a daily basis. Lord Carnarvon sells the rights to report on the tomb's contents to *The Times* in London to pay his researchers and to stop the flow of nosy journalists.

NEW DISCOVERY

news
EGYPT'S GREATEST

CURSE OF THE MUMMY

Lord Carnarvon dies from an insect bite six months after my tomb is uncovered. People mistake the spells in my tomb for evil curses and assume I am responsible. The "Curse of the Mummy" is born and my fame continues to spread.

KILLER BITE
KING TUTANKHAMUN CURSE

UP CLOSE AND PERSONAL WITH
KING TUTANKHAMUN

It's thanks to the Egyptian practice of mummification that my remains are so well preserved.

HOW TO MAKE A MUMMY

1 Make a slit in the side of the dead body and remove all internal organs, except the heart. Store organs in little canopic jars.

2 Insert a rod up the nose and break apart the brain. Drain through the nostrils.

3 Stuff and rub the body with natron, a kind of salt. Leave to dry for forty days.

4 Replace natron with sawdust and linen. Oil the skin and wrap with linen bandages.

GETTING UNDRESSED

When Carter discovers me, he and his helpers unwrap me entirely—from my outer shrine right down to my bandages. I am left wearing only my beaded skullcap and necklace (which can't be removed because they are stuck to my flesh). I feel very vulnerable.

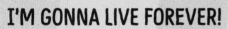

I'M GONNA LIVE FOREVER!

Although they cover me back up when visitors come through, Egyptologists still insist on undressing me again to take x-rays and CT scans—look at the state of me! I must admit though, I do like being on TV all the time. This is exactly what I always wanted—to be the most famous pharaoh of them all, and to live forever!

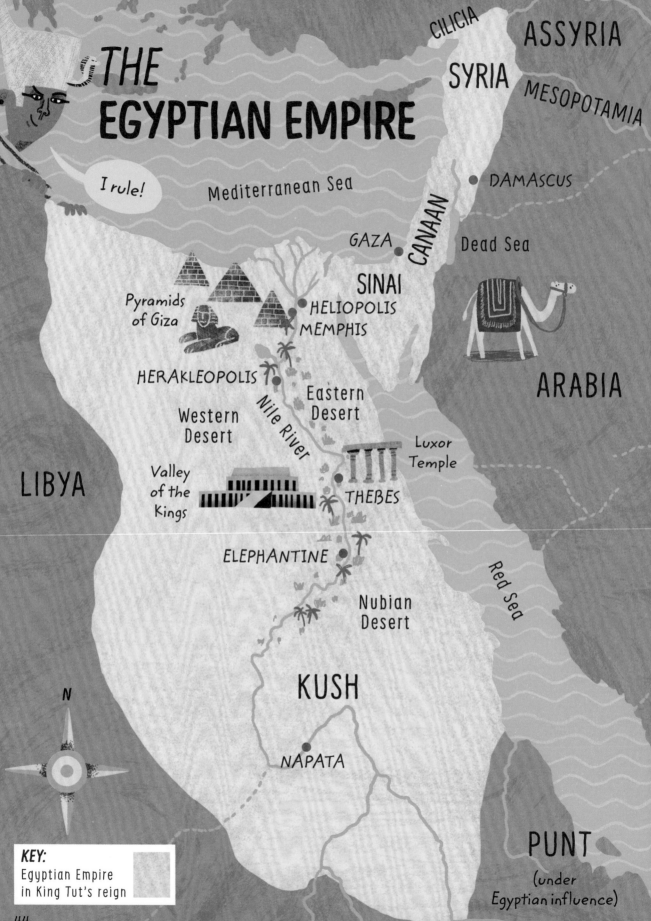

EGYPTIAN HIEROGLYPHS

Hieroglyphs are the picture symbols used to write things down in ancient Egypt, instead of letters. There are over 700 in total, so you have to be a clever scribe to know the meaning of them all.

HOW TO SAY MY NAME

The word you really need to learn is my name! It's made up of three Egyptian words: "tut," "ankh" and "Amun." "Tut" means "image." The "ankh" sign means "life" or "living." "Amun" is the name of our most important god. Altogether, my name means "the living image of Amun."

> It's true—I am godlike.

Amun   tut   ankh

SOME OF MY OTHER FAVORITE HIEROGLYPHS

MAN = SI

This is the sign for a man. It is written at the end of every man's name.

WOMAN = SIT

This is the sign for a woman. It is written at the end of every woman's name.

GODDESS = MAAT

This sign of a goddess has a feather on her head. It's Maat, who you met on page 29.

ARCHER = MESHA

This sign of an archer with a bow and arrow is also used to write words like "army."

CAT = MIW

The Egyptian word for cat is "miw"—the sound a cat makes!

OWL = EM

The owl sign is used to write the letter "m" and can mean "in," "at" or "as."

ELEPHANT = ABU

The elephant sign is used to write "ivory," the material elephant tusks are made of.

EYE OF HORUS = UDJAT

The eye of the god Horus is good luck. It means Horus is protecting you.

Glossary

18th Dynasty – the name Egyptologists give to the period of time when Tutankhamun and his family reigned, from c. 1539 BCE to 1292 BCE

afterlife – some religions believe that a person has a second life after they are dead, called the "afterlife"

anatomist – someone who studies the body and its parts

ancient Egypt – a civilization in northeastern Africa that is famous for its arts and monuments. It lasted for nearly 3,000 years, from 2925 BCE to 145 BCE.

archaeologist – someone who studies history by digging up objects from the ground and studying them

artisan – a person who is skilled at making something by hand

Book of the Dead, The – spells written on papyrus designed to protect a person on their journey to the afterlife

burial chamber – inside a tomb, this is the room where the mummy is placed

canopic jar – a container used in ancient Egypt to store the mummified organs of a dead body

club foot – a birth defect that causes a person's foot or feet to turn inwards, making walking difficult or painful. Today a club foot can be treated with therapy and a minor operation.

CT scan – a type of x-ray that takes detailed images of the inside of the body, including internal organs, blood vessels and bones. "CT" stands for "computerized tomography."

cult – a religious group that worships one person or object

Egyptologist – someone who studies ancient Egypt

embalm – to treat a dead body with chemicals to stop it from decaying

emmer – an ancient type of wheat used to make cereals, bread and beer

eternal – something that lasts forever

funeral mask – a mask used to cover the face of a dead person

funerary team – the group of people who organize someone's burial

genetics – the study of genes. Genes instruct the cells in your body how to grow and develop. Genes determine many things, including the color of your eyes and hair.

hieroglyphs – the picture symbols representing words and sounds that were using for writing in ancient Egypt

jackal – a wild dog found in Africa and southern Asia

mace – a stick for hitting people with

mummification – the process of creating a mummy from a dead body

mummy – a dead body that has been purified and embalmed to stop it from decaying

natron – a salt mixture used during the mummification process to dry out a dead body and stop it from decaying

papyrus – a paper-like material made from the papyrus plant, used in ancient Egypt

pectoral – a piece of jewelry worn on the chest

pharaoh – the ruler in ancient Egypt

pyramid – a monument used to mark the tomb of a dead person. Egypt's famous pyramids mark the tombs of royal people, but in the time of Tutankhamun pyramids usually marked the tombs of non-royals.

sarcophagus – a stone coffin

scarab beetle – also known as the "dung beetle." This insect feeds on balls of manure from other animals. In ancient Egypt the scarab beetle was a symbol for the sun god Ra.

scribe – a person whose job it is to write out official documents by hand

seal – a piece of wax or clay that is melted onto an envelope, rope or ribbon to seal it closed

shabti – a figurine buried in the tomb of a dead person in ancient Egypt

shrine – a shelter that holds the dead remains or statue of someone who is holy or important, like a god

spell book – a roll of papyrus with spells written on it

tomb raider – a person who breaks into a tomb and steals things from it

tunic – a piece of clothing that reaches from the shoulders to the waist, or to the knees

Index

DR. CHRIS NAUNTON is an Egyptologist and author from London, U.K., who is often on TV. He has written lots of books including *Searching for the Lost Tombs of Egypt* and *Egyptologists' Notebooks*. He has been to Egypt more times than he can count.

GUILHERME KARSTEN is an illustrator from Blumenau, Brazil, who has won many prestigious awards for his artwork. He is the author and illustrator of *Aaahhh!* and has illustrated over 30 books for children.

FSC
www.fsc.org
MIX
Paper from responsible sources
FSC® C008047

King Tutankhamun Tells All! © 2021 Thames & Hudson Ltd, London

Text © 2021 Chris Naunton
Illustrations © 2021 Guilherme Karsten

Designed by Sarah Malley

First published in the United States of America in 2021 by Thames & Hudson Inc., 500 Fifth Avenue, New York, New York 10110

Library of Congress Control Number: 2020949896

ISBN 978-0-500-65255-8

Printed and bound in China by C & C Offset Printing Co. Ltd

Be the first to know about our new releases, exclusive content and author events by visiting
thamesandhudson.com
thamesandhudsonusa.com
thamesandhudson.com.au

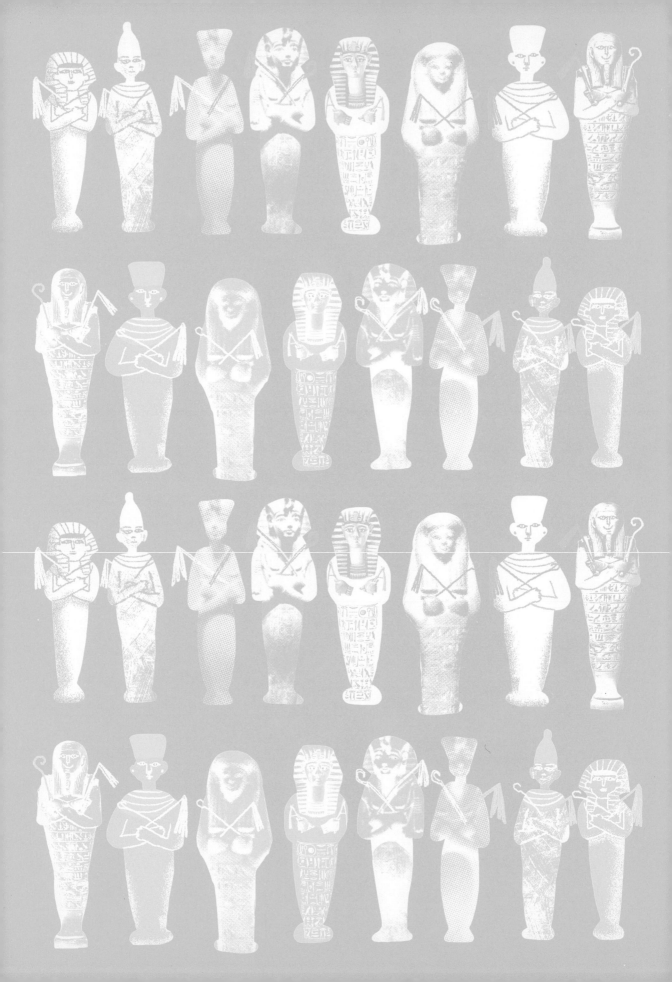